Calling Things That Are Not

by Charles Capps

*Unless otherwise indicated, all Scripture
quotations are taken from the King James
Version KJV of the Bible.*

23 22 21   05 04 03

Calling Things That Are Not
ISBN 13: 978-1-937578-31-2

Copyright © 2015 by Annette Capps
PO Box 69
England, Arkansas 72046

Published by Capps Publishing
PO Box 10,
Broken Arrow, OK 74013

www.cappsministries.com

Foreword by Annette Capps

It's been my privilege to watch the transformation that took place in my Dad's life after the Holy Spirit revealed the principle of "Calling Things".

One summer day I was summoned to the kitchen where the table was piled with notes and mortgages – debts owed to the bank. Dad said, "I want you to be a witness that I am going to do what Jesus said to do." He pointed his finger at the papers and said, "Notes, listen to me, I'm talking to you. Jesus said you would obey me. In the name of the Lord Jesus Christ, I command you, I say to you, BE PAID IN FULL . . . DEMATERIALIZE . . . DEPART . . . BE GONE . . . IN JESUS' NAME, YOU WILL OBEY ME!" Then, he just walked off. I stood there thinking, "I guess he just left to let those notes absorb his words?"

Those papers certainly looked like a mountain of debt to me but I really didn't doubt because I didn't expect that they had any choice but to obey the name of Jesus.

Next, we drove to the property that was security for the debt. Dad rolled down the window and shouted, "Listen to me! I am talking to you! Someone is impressed with you and you will be a blessing to someone. I call you "SOLD" in Jesus' name!" And then we drove off.

I later learned from him that when the property didn't sell right away and doubt began to enter his mind, he drove by the property again, rolled the window down, and said "Ha, ha, ha!", laughing at them and releasing faith that no matter what it looked like, the property was sold.

He called things that were not as though they were, calling the property sold and the debts paid until it manifest. Over the next few months, the property sold and all those notes and debts on the kitchen table were paid in full. Sure enough, debt was gone!

Annette Capps

Calling Things That Are Not

as Though They Were

There is no other subject that is more important to the Body of Christ today than the *Bible* principle of *calling things that are not.* Yet it is a subject that is very controversial in some religious circles and grossly misunderstood by many.

I admonish you to approach this subject with a desire to know and understand God's methods. They may seem strange to you because of your religious background. But don't make a decision for or against the subject until you know what God said and did concerning this matter.

This book is important to the rest of your life. Read it prayerfully. It is dedicated to your freedom and success, both spiritually and financially.

For ye see your calling, brethren, how that not many wise men after the flesh, not many mighty, not many noble, are called:

But God hath chosen the foolish things of the world to confound the wise; and God hath chosen the weak things of the world to confound the things which are mighty;

And base things of the world, and things which are despised, hath God chosen, yea, and *things which are not, to bring to nought things that are.*

I Corinthians 1:26-28

God has chosen this method. Some don't know this scripture is in the Bible, even though they have read it many times. God chose this method of using things that are not manifest (things that you cannot see with the natural eye) *to bring to nought the things that are manifest. Nought* means "zero"; "to bring to nought" means to reduce to nothing the things that are manifest.

This is a Bible principle. God chose it. I didn't choose it until after God chose it. God could have done it any way He wanted to, but He chose to do it this way. He chose to use things that are not manifest. He chose spiritual forces that you cannot see, feel, taste, smell or hear to bring to nought the things that are manifest. He chose this method to reduce to nought those things that are not in agreement with the Word of God. If you have a problem and you can see it, then it's in the natural realm. As long as you can see it, you can use your faith and the Word of God to change it.

We having the same spirit of faith, according as it is written, I believed, and therefore have I spoken; we also believe, and therefore speak....

For our light affliction, which is but for a moment, worketh for us a far more exceeding and eternal weight of glory;

While we look not at the things which are seen, but at the things which are not seen: for the things which are seen are temporal; but the things which are not seen are eternal.

2 Corinthians 4:13, 17-18

The unseen realm is the powerful realm. The unseen is governed by God's eternal principles. Here is the principle that God has ordained. God used it all through the Bible, from Genesis to Revelation. It's the principle that Jesus used in all of His ministry. It's the principle of calling things that are not as though they were. We find Paul's account of God doing this in Romans 4.

> **(As it is written, I have made thee a father of many nations,) before him whom he believed, even God, who quickeneth the dead, and calleth those things which be not as though they were.**
>
> Romans 4:17

God calls things that are not manifest as though they were manifest. Compare this with what the Apostle Paul said, "God has chosen the *things which are not, to bring to nought things that are.*" (1 Cor. 1:28.) This is God's method. Call for eternal forces that put to nought things that are seen. Call into manifestation the things that are not, and they will replace what is manifest.

Paul said that we should overcome evil with good. When you start talking about calling things that are not as though they were, *some people get the idea you are denying what exists.* Some believe that confessing the answer is denying the things that exist. But confessing the answer is not denying what exists; it is the principle of calling things that are not as though they were.

Don't Call Things That *Are* As Though They Were *Not*

There is a great difference between calling things that are not as though they were and calling things that are as though they are not. God's method is to call things that are not. In other words, He calls them into manifestation. By doing that, He nullifies the problem that exists.

If the problem exists, you don't deny that the problem exists. If you are sick, you don't deny that you are sick. But on the other hand you don't want to always be confessing your sickness either. Some who misunderstand this message think if they are sick, they should say, ''I'm not sick." Just denying you are sick won't make you well. In fact, that could be a lie. But there is a difference between a lie and a confession.

Confession is a method of calling things that are not as though they were. If I am sick, I will confess:

> *I am healed by the stripes of Jesus. I am delivered from the authority of darkness. I am redeemed from the curse of the law. I am calling my body well and healthy in Jesus' name.*

I am not denying sickness; I am denying its right to exist in my body. I am calling for health and healing in my body. That is God's method.

There are those who will say, "You are just trying to act like God."

And I appreciate that; I usually say, "Thank you very much."

I would rather act like God than act like the devil. If I am acting like God, saying what God said about me, then those who are saying what the devil said are acting like the devil.

If you are always quoting what the devil said, then you are agreeing with the devil. The devil will tell you, "You're sick, and you are going to die. You are never going to get any better."

Well, it may look that way on the surface, but don't quote the devil - he is a liar. Even when there is no hope, don't confess no hope, but go to God's Word and get some hope.

When there was no hope, *Abraham believed in hope.* He took God's Word for his hope. He began to say what God said about him. "I am the father of many nations." God forced him into it by changing his name. He had to say, "My name is Abraham," and *Abraham* meant "father of many nations."

Faith comes by hearing the Word of God. That was the Word of God concerning Abraham: *"You are the father of nations."* But he wasn't the father of nations at that time. *But God said he was.* What was God doing? He was calling for it. God taught Abraham to say what He said by changing his name from Abram to Abraham.

God also spoke to Zacharias, but the reaction was not the same.

...the angel said unto him, Fear not, Zacharias: for thy prayer is heard; and thy wife Elisabeth shall bear thee a son, and thou shalt call his name John....

And Zacharias said unto the angel, Whereby shall I know this? For I am an old man and my wife well stricken in years.

And the angel answering said unto him, I am Gabriel, that stand in the presence of God; and am sent to speak unto thee, and to shew thee these glad tidings.

And, behold, thou shalt be dumb, and not able to speak, until the day that these things shall be performed, because thou believest not my words, which shall be fulfilled in their season.

Luke 1:13, 18-20

Allow me to paraphrase this. God sent an angel to Zacharias to tell him that his prayers were answered, and his wife was going to have a child. Zacharias said, "How do I know you're telling the truth? You'll have to give me a sign."

The angel replied, "I'll give you a sign all right. You won't be able to speak until the day it comes to pass."

Notice how God dealt with these two individuals, Abraham and Zacharias. Here was a man who was walking in doubt concerning what God said to him. So God seemed to say, *"If we don't get his mouth shut, this will never happen."*

So the angel stopped Zacharias from talking for nine months. But God renamed Abraham, so he would have to say what God said about him.

Remember that God chose this method of calling things that are not as though they were. But there are some who misunderstand and deny what exists. For instance, someone might say, "I'm going to deny that I have emphysema," and continue to confess that they don't have emphysema.

If they could get rid of it by denying it, they might still die with cancer. So that's not the answer. *God's method is to call the thing that is not as though it were. That does not mean to deny what exists.* You don't call things that *are* as though they are not. *God's method is to call things that are not manifest as though they were manifest.*

Confession Is Not a Lie

If you were going to apply God's principles concerning sickness, you would say,

> *Thank God, the Bible says that I am healed by the stripes of Jesus. I am redeemed from the curse of the law. The curse of the law was poverty, sickness and spiritual death. First Peter 2:24 says that I was healed by the stripes of Jesus, and I am confessing these things and saying them in the name of Jesus.*
>
> *It is causing faith to come, and I am calling my body well. Body, are you listening to me? I am telling you that you are well in the name of Jesus.*

Then someone may say, "I know that you are just lying, because you are hurting."

I may be hurting, but I am calling for the thing that is not manifest.

10

"How can you say your body is well when you are sick?"

That's all the more reason that you should say it. You are calling for the thing that you don't have. You are calling it into manifestation. There would be no need to call for something that was already manifest.

I am not trying to convince you that I am not sick, or that I am not hurting. If I were, I would be lying. There is a difference between lying and confession, or calling things that are not. If I try to convince you that I already have something that I don't literally have, then it's a lie. But if you hear me saying, "Thank God, my body is well, I am healed, I am delivered, I am free from sickness and disease, and I am calling my body well," you just heard me calling things that are not. I did not lie to you. I wasn't talking to you. I didn't say it for your benefit; I said it for my benefit. I would rather that you had not heard me, because you are likely to misunderstand me. I am calling for the things that are not manifest until they are manifest.

Use Common Sense

Someone might say, "Thank God, I am going to confess that I don't have any debts," when in fact, they owe everybody in the county. There are many people who are hung up on this scripture in Romans 13:8, **Owe no man any thing, but to love one another**.... They say, "Glory to God, that's what I'm going to do. I am going to owe no man anything." If they get behind on their bills, they won't borrow money to meet their obligations. They lose their credit and get kicked out of their apartment.

That is not a very good testimony. They are confessing, "My God meets my needs according to His riches in glory." The other people are wondering, "Who is his God Who can't meet his needs?"

You can't be debt free and owe everybody at the same time. You have to start where you are. What I am saying is that you cannot operate in that until you get out of debt. Don't get into bondage over that scripture. God told Israel in Deuteronomy 15:6 **... thou shalt lend unto many nations, but thou shalt not borrow**.... If it were wrong to borrow money, it would be wrong to

12

lend money. For they wouldn't have borrowed if there had not been someone to lend it.

If God has told you not to borrow money, then it would be wrong for you to do it. But don't get into bondage over that one verse of scripture. Quite frankly, this scripture in Romans 13:8 is talking about paying your taxes.

For this cause pay ye tribute also: for they are God's ministers, attending continually upon this very thing.

Render therefore to all their dues: tribute to whom tribute is due; custom to whom custom; fear to whom fear; honour to whom honour. Owe no man any thing, but to love one another: for he that loveth another hath fulfilled the law.

Romans 13:6-8

In other words, if someone is worthy of honor, give it to them. Give tribute and custom—don't withhold it. In other words, pay your income tax.

But what if someone said, "I don't have any debts. Glory to God, I don't have any

13

debts. I am confessing that every bill is paid. I don't have any debts," when, in fact, they owe many people? They are denying what exists; they are calling things that *are* as though they are *not*. That is not God's method. God's method is to call for the thing that is *not* manifest. Even if they could eliminate the debt by denying its existence, they might starve to death. Most people who starve to death don't owe anybody anything. So, just being out of debt is not the answer.

What is the answer? God's method is to call the thing that is not manifest. The thing that is not manifest in that individual's life is an abundant supply. So that person should go to the Word and find the promise of abundant supply, then be obedient to what the Word said to do to activate the promise. Then they should proclaim —

I have given and it is given unto me; good measure, pressed down, and shaken together, and running over. My God supplies all my need according to His riches in glory by Christ Jesus.

14

Because I am a giver, because I operate on the principles of the Word of God, I sow bountifully, and I reap bountifully. My God has made all grace abound toward me.

I am saying in the name of Jesus that I have abundance, and all the good deals come my way. I am blessed going in and coming out. I am blessed in the basket and in the store. By the end of the year I will have abundance to meet my obligations and give ten thousand dollars to missions.

If someone heard you confessing abundance, they might say, "I know you are lying, because I happen to know that you don't have the money for your car payment."

That's all the more reason for saying it. You are calling the thing that is not yet manifest.

Apply the Principle and Be Patient

It may take weeks, months or years to bring the total fulfillment of that promise. But then you will be able to pay your debts, buy groceries and give to missions.

Let's say it another way. There is a backlash in denying what exists. A man says, "I found the car I want to buy. If I sell my car, I will have enough money to buy this car." But he misunderstood the faith message, so he begins to deny that he has a car. He says, "I believe I have sold my car, so I am going to deny that I have a car." So he starts saying, "I don't have a car. I don't have a car." Somebody asks him about his car and he says, "I don't have a car."

He may wake up some morning and find that someone has stolen his car, and he really doesn't have a car. So that is not the answer. There is a backlash in denying things that exist. That is not faith, neither is it God's method.

God's method would be to say something like this.

Father, in the name of Jesus, I ask You for a buyer for this car. Send someone to buy this car. Someone wants this car. This car will fill the need in someone's life, and they want it as badly as I want to sell it.

Send them to me, Father. Have the angels guide them here. I thank You, Father. I believe that I have received a buyer for this car. Thank You, Father, that my car is sold.

Then go out and talk to your car. Say, "Car, I am calling you sold. Someone loves your paint job. They are impressed with you. By faith I call you sold, in Jesus' name."

How do you know that you are not lying?

Because you are calling things that are not. Although the car is still in your possession, you are taking the spiritual force of faith and calling into manifestation the thing that will nullify what exists. *When you call health into your body, it will nullify sickness and disease. Call abundance into your finances, and it will nullify lack.* It will nullify the thing that exists.

There is probably no other principle in the Bible that will cause you to be criticized more than this one. But yet it is God's method. There are so many Christians who simply don't understand this principle.

Acting as God Would Act

Some will accuse you of trying to be God. They will say, "You are trying to act like God."

But you are only trying to *act as God would act if He were in your situation. You are not trying to be God.* If God had a car to sell, He would call it sold. For in Genesis 1:2, 3 when He saw darkness, He said, *"Light!"* God speaks the thing desired. He calls the thing that is not manifest and brings to nothing the thing that is manifest. I didn't invent this method. But I found it in the Bible and have proven it in my own life.

Let's consider how the principle would work regarding everyday situations. I heard one lady say, "Pray for my husband. I've been praying for him for twenty-five years, and he's getting worse, he won't go to church with me."

She had been praying that way all those years. She had been telling the Lord that her husband was getting worse and that he wouldn't go to church with her. She prayed the problem for twenty-five years. If she had prayed the answer and called for the thing that was not, no doubt her husband would have been saved more than twenty years ago.

But she was calling things that were as though they were. This is another mistake many Christians make. They call things that are as though they are, and they establish the present circumstances. Why would you call something that was already manifest? People do foolish things sometimes, thinking they are being spiritual. They say, "I'm just telling it like it is. You have to say it like it is."

But calling things that *are manifest* is not God's method. The Bible method is to *call the things that are not manifest* and keep calling them until they are manifest.

Don't Make a Habit of Confessing Your Weakness

Say unto wisdom, Thou art my sister; and call understanding thy kinswoman.

Proverbs 7:4

Someone might say, "I never know what to do." They are probably right; especially if they

19

have been saying that for twenty years. They have shut off the wisdom of God from their spirit by the words of their mouth. In this scripture, *God is telling you to call wisdom and understanding.* If you want wisdom, call for wisdom. Proclaim that you have the wisdom of God.

If you always make dumb decisions, *begin to confess you have the wisdom of God.* Don't say it like it is. Say it the way you want it to be, based on the Word.

It is foolish to confess, "I make dumb decisions, I always make dumb decisions." Many do it just that way, thinking they are being honest. People will tell you that you have to say it like it is. Some say, —

I'm just saying it like it is. I don't ever have enough money to give in the offering. I'm not able to give to missions because money gets away from me so quickly that I don't ever know where it goes. I just can't keep money.

Isn't that amazing? They have been saying that for twenty-nine years. And money just flees from them and seems to disappear.

If that has been your experience, start confessing this instead.

I always have enough money for every good work. There is abundance and no lack. My money multiplies every month and stays with me. I always have sufficient funds because I am a giver.

But don't go tell your neighbors that, because they may call you a liar. But you are renewing your mind and causing faith to come.

There is a fine line here. This is between you and God. *You proclaim these things based on the Scriptures.* It is not a matter of whether or not it exists now. It's a matter of what you can call into existence by the Word of God and your confession of faith in God's promises.

A Divine Principle

Calling things that are not is a Bible method. It is a divine Bible principle.

Remember now, we are not calling things that *are as though they are not,* for that would be denying what exists. Denying what exists is not God's method.

God's method is to call for the things God has promised in His Word, although they are not manifest yet.

There are some who will say, "I don't believe in calling things that are not." But if you follow that individual around, you will find they are doing it almost every day. They will say, "You watch and see. That car is going to pull right out in front of us." "I can already tell that we are not going to have the money to make our house payment this month." "If you buy that car, sure as the world you'll lose your job."

These are the people who will criticize you for calling things that are not as though they were, *on the positive side.*

Worry is simply calling things that are not as though they were, on the negative side. But when we start doing this on the positive side, religious people get upset about it. They say, "Why, you're just trying to live in a world of fantasy." But yet they will stand there and call things that are not, on the negative side, and say, "Well, I'm just saying it like it is. I'm being truthful." They don't know they are deceived.

It may be true all right, but we are not required to call something that is already there. That is not God's method. They are calling the bad things that are not as though they were. If they continue to do that, they will call them into manifestation. The thing they greatly feared will come upon them, just as it happened to Job.[1]

Acting on Scripture

Calling things that are not is acting on Mark 11:23: **... whosoever shall say unto this mountain, Be thou removed, and be thou cast into the sea... shall have whatsoever he saith.** If you are saying to the mountain, "Be thou removed," you are doing it on the positive side. You will probably be criticized. But the same people who criticize you are talking to the same mountain and saying, *"Whoooo, mountain, you are getting bigger every day. I'll never get over you. You are always there to hinder me."*

They will criticize you even though they are using the same principle, only in reverse.

---

[1] The CD "What About Job" by Charles Capps explores this subject in greater depth.

There are some who say, "You are denying what exists if you call things that are not."

No, we are not denying the things that exist. *We are doing something about what exists by calling something in its place.* You notice in the Scriptures that God taught Abraham *His* method of calling things that are not. And Abraham did not deny what existed, but rather gave affirmation to what God said about him.

Abraham did not say, "I am not old, I am not old, I am not old." He didn't deny that he was old. He was seventy-five years old when God told him that He would make of him a great nation. (Gen. 12:24.) Then God appeared to Abram again in Genesis 17:1-12 and changed his name to Abraham which meant "Father of Nations" or "Father of a Multitude."

Through this name change God forced Abraham to tell everyone he was the father of nations. Yet it was twenty-five years later when he became the father of nations in the natural. *He had God's promise for twenty-five years,* and he was getting older all the time. He was too old to father a child when God told him he was the father of many nations. He did not deny that he was old, but rather gave the positive affirmation in agreement with God. When he said, "I am Abraham," he was saying, "I am the father of nations." After he began to say what God had said, it was less than a year until the promised child was born. Faith cometh by hearing.

God has revealed some things to us about faith in the New Covenant that He did not reveal to Abraham. It is important to know how to operate in these principles. If we don't know and understand these principles, we are likely to deny what exists. But through this principle we don't deny what exists, we just don't give it first place. Don't continually talk about what exists, especially if it doesn't agree with God's Word. For the more you talk it, *the more you will believe it.* The more you believe it, the more you will talk it. *Both faith and fear come by hearing.*

The principle that God has chosen uses things that are not manifest *to bring to nought things that are manifest.* But yet you hear some say, "I'm going to say it like it is; that's the way you have to do it. If I say it any other way, I would be lying, so I always just say it like it is."

But When It Comes to Cats and Dogs, They Do It Differently

Let's see if that is really true in their life. Let's suppose that person has a dog, and it's time to feed him. They take the food out some morning, and the dog isn't there. If they really practice what they say they believe — (that you have to say it like it is) — here is what they will do. They will sit down on the doorstep and start saying, "My dog isn't here, my dog isn't here. Oh Lord, my dog is gone. Oh, it's true, the dog isn't here."

They groan all morning saying, "The dog's not here."

Finally, their neighbor comes over and says, "What are you doing?"

They reply, "Well, just saying it like it is. The dog is not here. The dog is gone."

The neighbor says, "Have you tried calling the dog?"

They reply, *"No! You can't do that. You have to say it like it is, and the dog is not here. The dog is gone."*

It is true that the dog is not there. And the dog may never be there, unless they call him. No one would ever think of doing such a thing. It's ridiculous. No one would do that in natural things.

You know what they would do if they went out to feed the dog and the dog wasn't there? They would say, "Here pooch! Here pooch!" — even though pooch was not there.

Are they lying about it when they say, "Here pooch! Here pooch!" when the pooch is not here? They say that they always say it like it is, but if they are going to say it like it is, they should say, "Yonder pooch! Yonder pooch! Somewhere pooch!" But when it comes to cats and dogs, no one would be that foolish.

Why is it, when we get into the Bible in regard to these principles, we forget about cats and dogs or natural things? For the simple reason that *we have totally separated natural principles from spiritual principles.* We shouldn't do that, because there are parallels between the two. Whatever you call in the natural will come. When you plant a seed, you are calling for more seed. Seedtime and harvest is God's method. Planting a seed calls for the things that are not there at the time.

Saying It Like It Is, or Saying It like It Is Not

You would call the dog, "Here pooch! Here pooch!" until pooch comes. Remember, when it comes to dogs and cats, even the person who says he believes in calling it like it is *calls the thing that is not there.* Suppose he goes out to feed the dog, and the dog is there. So he sits down and says, "Here's pooch! Here's pooch! Pooch is here; here's pooch!" His neighbor comes over and says, "What are you doing?"

He replies, "I'm just saying it like it is. Pooch is here, so I am calling pooch here."

No one would do that. There is no need to call the dog, if the dog is already there. Everybody knows the dog is there.

Here is the point I want to make. Some people say, "We are so financially strapped we will never be able to buy anything that we need. We always have month left at the end of our money. We can never keep money. Every time we save any money, our kids get sick and we have to spend every dime on doctor bills. We always get the flu in January every year."

What are they doing? They are calling things *that are already there.* They are establishing what already exists.

They wouldn't do that to their dog. They wouldn't do that to their cat. Why are they doing that concerning things they don't want? They don't want lack in their house. They don't want poverty on their doorstep. They don't want sickness in their family. So why would they continue to call it the way it is? Why not *call it the way the Bible says it should be?* Call for the thing desired, the thing God promised. *Use God's method to change what exists.*

Remember, God chose this method. You can choose whatever method you want to in life. But you will have better success if you go with God's method.

There are many who will disagree with you. They will say you are lying. But if you bring it back to cats and dogs, you will find they are using God's principles in natural things. But when it comes to spiritual things, they are so heavenly minded that they are no earthly good. They get confused because they haven't studied and meditated on these Bible principles.

In natural things, you wouldn't call something that was already manifest. If you wanted the dog and the cat was there, *you would stomp your foot and say, "Scat!" and then call the dog.* If lack has come home with you tell lack to *go* in the name of Jesus! Call abundance by confessing the Word of God. *Don't sit there and call it like it is.* Call it the way God promised it would be. *Call the promise into manifestation.*

Call Things Desired

In the area of sickness and disease, *you call the thing that is desired.*

...What things soever ye desire, when ye pray, believe that ye receive them, and ye shall have them.

Mark 11:24

Notice the phrase, *you shall have them.* It's foolish in the natural realm to call something that you already have. You would call the thing that was not there. It's a simple principle. It is so simple that we have missed it. This principle is used throughout the Bible. God started it and operated in it. *Jesus operated in it during all of His earthly ministry.* It is one of the most tremendous truths in the whole Bible. But because we have been taught wrong, the devil has blinded our minds to some of these things. The enemy has convinced so many that they are lying when they call things that are not as though they were.

If you call the cat or dog that is not there, they will obey you and come. Someone may say, "I can understand that cat and dog business, but talking to your body and calling it well, that's just too far out." Do you mean to tell me that the cat and dog are smarter than your body?

Jesus said in Mark 11:23 that a man shall have whatever he says if he believes and doubts not in his heart, but shall believe what he is saying will come to pass. *He shall have whatever he says.*

He is telling you how to call the thing that is not. You say to the mountain while it is still standing there, "Be removed, be cast into the sea." You say to the sycamine tree, "Be plucked up by the root, be planted in the sea." You are calling it the way you want it, according to the Scriptures. The mountain of problem must obey. It has no other choice.

The promises in the Bible are God's will for you. But they will not come to you just because they are in the Bible. You must call them. Check up on yourself. You have been calling things for years, and that is the reason you are in the situation you are in. *You have been calling the wrong things.* You have been calling things that are not, but doing it on the negative side. To change your situation, all you have to do is switch over to the positive side of the same principle.

The Power of God's Word Over All Matter

Some say, "That's just positive thinking or mind over matter."

No. *It's the principle of God and the power of His Word over all matter.* It's God's method. We are created in the image of God and we can operate in His principles.

You must have some understanding to operate in these principles. If you don't have a good understanding, people will talk you out of it. They will tell you that you are not operating in Bible principles, that you're just lying.

They don't know this is God's way. *If they could just live a few days in it, they would never go back to their way.* But their eyes have been blinded, and their words have deceived their hearts.

Learn to call things that are not as though they were. This is God's method of nullifying what exists, by calling into manifestation the thing that the Bible promised.

33

We are talking about calling the promises of God. It is not something that God doesn't want you to have, *but things that God has already given to you.*

Jesus Called the Water Wine

Jesus operated in this principle of "calling things" throughout His ministry on earth. In John the second chapter we find the account of the marriage in Cana of Galilee where they ran out of wine.

His mother saith unto the servants, whatsoever he saith unto you, do it.

And there were set there six waterpots of stone, after the manner of the purifying of the Jews, containing two or three firkins apiece.

Jesus saith unto them, Fill the waterpots with water. And they filled them up to the brim.

And he saith unto them, Draw out now, and bear unto the governor of the feast. And they bare it.

John 2:5-8

They filled the water pots to the brim with water. It was water. It wasn't coffee. It wasn't grape juice. It was water. They knew it was water, John knew it was water. Peter knew it was water, Jesus knew it was water.

But Jesus called it wine. You need to understand that Jesus was more highly developed in this than you. Jesus spoke only what His Father said. You can see the principle here. I am not telling you to go out and try to turn water into gasoline.

The point that I am making is that this is a principle. It works in everything in life. He is not telling you to go turn water into wine, or wine into water. But this Bible principle can be used to supply your need.

Jesus said:
...Draw out now, and bear unto the governor of the feast. And they bare it.

John 2:8

Some will tell you, "You are just playing make-believe, confessing all these things. You're just living in a world of make-believe."

35

What does the scripture say? Does it say, "This is the beginning of make-believe which Jesus did?" No it doesn't say that. It says,

This beginning of miracles did Jesus in Cana of Galilee....
John 2:11

People may tell you that you are playing make-believe. They may tell you all sorts of things. Religious people who are dogmatic about their own little doctrines are the most vicious people in the world.

Obey the principle. Don't try to turn water into gasoline or wine. Call for what is needed in your life. Jesus didn't just sit there and say, "We can't have wine. We don't have wine." He called for some water, and it came. Then He called it wine. *He used what was available to call the thing that was needed.* Water, which was not wine, brought to nought the need, which was wine.

Jesus Called the Crooked Straight

In Luke 13, Jesus was in the synagogue.

And, behold, there was a woman which had a spirit of infirmity eighteen years, and was bowed together, and could in no wise lift up herself.

And when Jesus saw her, he called her to him, and said unto her, Woman, thou art loosed from thine infirmity.

Luke 13:11-12

Jesus called her loosed, but she wasn't loosed. She was still as bent over as she ever was. What was Jesus doing? Was He playing make-believe? No. He was calling for the thing that was not manifest. He was calling for a miracle.

As you study the Bible, you will notice God never does anything until He says it. That's the way He works. God has done nothing in the earth without first speaking it. Even now, it seems that God will do nothing in the earth unless it is spoken, prophesied or called for by the prayer of faith.

When Isaiah prophesied that a virgin would conceive and bear a child, that was 750 years before Jesus was born in the earth.

37

It was prophesied. God always prophesies it before it happens. Jesus operated in the same principle. He walked up to that little woman and said, *"You are loosed from your infirmity."* But when He said that, she wasn't loosed. He was calling for the thing that was not manifest.

And he laid his hands on her: and immediately she was made straight, and glorified God.

Luke 13:13

First, Jesus called her the way He wanted her to be. Faith always looks through the storm. *Faith always sees the end results.* When Jesus walked up to this woman, He could see the end results by His faith, so He just called her the way He saw her by faith, loosed from that infirmity.

Jesus Called the Dead Living

Let's look at the story of Lazarus of Bethany in John eleven.

Therefore his sisters sent unto him, saying, Lord, behold, he whom thou lovest is sick.

**When Jesus heard that, he said, This
sickness is not unto death, but for the
glory of God, that the Son of God might
be glorified thereby.**

John 11:3-4

Jesus said, *"This sickness is not unto death."*
What are you going to do with that statement? For
as you read further, you find that Lazarus died.

Jesus said that this sickness was not unto
death but for the glory of God, that the Son
of God might be glorified thereby. Some say,
"Jesus said that Lazarus was sick and died so
God would be glorified."

It wasn't God's will for Lazarus to be sick.
Neither was it God's will for Lazarus to die.

Let me show you why you cannot interpret
this scripture to mean the sickness or death
was for God's glory. One of the rules of
interpretation is to always take a scripture
literally if you can. But you cannot take verse
four literally. If you do, you make Jesus a liar.
But there is a difference between a lie and a
confession, or calling things that are not. If
you interpret this verse literally, then you

would have to say Jesus lied. But a lie is sin, and the Bible says there was no sin in Him. So we have to look at it from a different angle.

Jesus Called End Results

Jesus is calling the end results of the matter. He said that the end result would not be death; but that *the end results of this whole matter would bring glory to God.* The glory that God received came when Lazarus was raised from the dead. Not when he was sick, nor when he died. Neither the sickness nor the death glorified God. *The resurrection glorified God.* God raised him from the dead. If it was God's will for Lazarus to die, then Jesus destroyed the work of His Father when He raised him from the dead. But Jesus came **...that he might destroy the works of the devil** (1 John 3:8). So Jesus destroyed the works of the devil when He raised Lazarus from the dead.

If you follow Jesus, you will learn something, as He starts toward Bethany.

Jesus Was Misunderstood Because of His Confession

These things said he: and after that he saith unto them, Our friend Lazarus *sleepeth*; but I go, that I may awake him out of sleep.

Then said his disciples, Lord, if he sleep, he shall do well.

Howbeit Jesus spake of his death: but they thought that he had spoken of taking of rest in sleep.

John 11:11-13

Jesus realized they had misunderstood Him when the disciples said, "If Lazarus is asleep, he is doing well." Jesus was calling the thing that was not. Lazarus wasn't asleep, he was dead, and Jesus knew he was dead. It took the runner about a day to get down there with the bad news. Then Jesus stayed there two more days, and then walked to Bethany, which took about one day. On the way to Bethany, Jesus said, *"Lazarus sleepeth."*

What was He doing? He was guarding His conversation so He wouldn't undo what He had already declared in the beginning *("The end results will not be death")*. But His disciples misunderstood Him.

Jesus Explained What Was, But Called What Was Not

Jesus stopped and gave His followers an explanation, **Lazarus is dead** (v. 14). That's the way the *King James Version* states it. But if you read the *Interlinear Greek-English New Testament*, the word translated **dead** in the *King James Version* is translated *died*.[2] One is present tense; the other is past tense. Jesus said, "Lazarus died." There is a difference between someone who died and someone who is dead. If you don't understand that, look at Jesus. He died, *but He is not dead*.

Jesus called the thing that was not manifest. Lazarus was not asleep. He was dead. But Jesus called him *"asleep."* Jesus would not admit

2   George Ricker Berry (Grand Rapids: Baker Book House, 1897)" p. 278

death. That didn't mean that He denied it. He just would not establish anything but what He declared when He heard the bad news.

Again, in this principle, Jesus is not teaching you to go raise all the dead. He is teaching you how the principle of calling things that are not works.

When Jesus came to Bethany, He said,

... Take ye away the stone. Martha, the sister of him that was dead, saith unto him, Lord, by this time he stinketh: for he hath been dead four days.

John 11:39

This fact that he had been dead for four days proves that he was either dead when the messenger got to Jesus, or died immediately after. For when Jesus arrived, they said that Lazarus had been dead four days. Jesus knew Lazarus was dead.

Jesus finally talked them into rolling away the stone.

Then they took away the stone from the place where the dead was laid. And

**Jesus lifted up his eyes, and said, Father,
I thank thee that thou hast heard me.**

John 11:41

Notice at this point, Jesus hasn't said anything yet, but He is thanking God that He has heard Him. Jesus is referring to what He said four days ago. In effect, He was saying, *"Father, I thank You that You heard what I decreed by faith four days ago; that the end results will not end in death but bring glory to You."*

Obeying the Principle

We must learn to obey this principle.

If someone calls and says, "Aunt Susie is in the hospital, and she's going to die for sure," use your faith to the limit. Dare to say some things in faith. Say, "In the name of Jesus, I believe she will live and not die. I decree it in Jesus' name."

"But what if she dies?"

Well, you used your faith to the limit. You did what you could.

There are some things you can't control by your faith. Aunt Susie might have wanted to go on to heaven, and you couldn't stop her. If she wants to go, you shouldn't stop her.

These are some things we need to understand. Don't get under condemnation for using your faith. Someone might say, "But I prayed for somebody, and they died."

What does that have to do with it? You are required to use your faith, but you can't control every situation or every circumstance.

I'd sure hate to be a partner to anyone dying before their time. But if an individual wants to go, you shouldn't always try to stop them. They should have the right to go home.

Jesus Established End Results

At the tomb of Lazarus, Jesus said to the Father, **...I thank thee that thou hast heard me.** He has established something.

And I knew that thou hearest me always: but because of the people which stand by I said it, that they may believe that thou hast sent me.

John 11:42

He said, *"I knew You would hear Me. That's the reason I said it. I wanted to establish this on earth."*

Psalm 119:89 says, **Forever, O Lord, thy word is settled in heaven.**

God's Word is already established in heaven; but on earth is where it needs to be established now. Look at what Jesus said to Peter:

And I will give unto thee the keys of the kingdom of heaven: and whatsoever thou shalt bind on earth shall be bound in heaven: and whatsoever thou shalt loose on earth shall be loosed in heaven.

Matthew 16:19

Jesus said the power of binding and loosing is on earth. You have authority to bind on earth those things which have been bound out of heaven. You can loose some things and they will be loosed -not only by you, but God in heaven will loose some things, if you will loose them. But you must do something first on earth. Jesus loosed Lazarus from death.

And when he thus had spoken, he cried with a loud voice, Lazarus, come forth.

John 11:43

I can just imagine what Peter was thinking when Jesus started talking to the dead. I imagine Peter was embarrassed.

Jesus Spoke to Things and They Obeyed

You will notice that in Jesus' ministry, He talked to trees. He talked to the wind. He talked to the sea. He talked to dead people. And they all obeyed Him. In every instance, He was calling for things that were not manifest.

When Lazarus came forth, I can see John nudging Peter and saying, "Hey, look, Peter! There is Lazarus standing in the door of the tomb!"

Then all embarrassment was gone. You may be embarrassed sometimes about some of the things you are saying, because it took so long for them to happen. But when you call the promise of God into manifestation in your life, all the embarrassment will leave.

Jesus Called for Peace in the Storm

Then again in Mark, chapter four, we find Jesus calling things that are not manifest.

And the same day, when the even was come, he saith unto them, Let us pass over unto the other side.

And there arose a great storm of wind, and the waves beat into the ship, so that it was now full.

And he was in the hinder part of the ship, asleep on a pillow: and they awake him, and say unto him, Master, carest thou not that we perish?

And he arose, and rebuked the wind, and said unto the sea, Peace, be still. And the wind ceased, and there was a great calm.

Mark 4:35, 37-39

Notice, Jesus spoke to the wind and the waves. As He stood up in the boat, He saw the wind boisterous and the waves coming into the boat. There was a real storm on the sea. He looked at the storm and said, *"Peace, be still."*

There wasn't any peace when He said that. But He was calling the thing that was not manifest. *"Peace, be still!"* sounds like a lie, doesn't it? There was no peace and nothing out there was still. *But He called it.*

I'm glad some of the people I know weren't in that boat. They would have said, "But, Jesus, You can't do that. You have to say it like it is." Wouldn't it have been foolish to stand up in that boat and say, "Big waves and strong winds! We're sinking!"?

Many people operate this principle that Jesus used in reverse to *prophesy their own doom.*

Jesus Called the Lepers Clean

Jesus called things that were not, in all of His ministry. He taught us to do the same. In Luke seventeen, we find the story of the ten lepers who cried out for Jesus to have mercy on them.

And as he entered into a certain village, there met him ten men that were lepers, which stood afar off:

49

And they lifted up their voices, and said, Jesus, Master, have mercy on us.

And when he saw them, he said unto them, Go shew yourselves unto the priests. And it came to pass, that, as they went, they were cleansed.

Luke 17:12-14

Notice that Jesus said, *"Go show yourselves to the priests."*

What was He talking about? Didn't He know they were lepers?

Yes, Jesus knew they were lepers. *But He was calling them clean.* The only scriptural reason they would show themselves to the priests was if they were cleansed. So Jesus was calling them clean. They could have said, "But Jesus, we don't believe in this calling things that are not. We don't believe in confessing something that is not already true. We just believe in saying it like it is. We call things as they are."

Had they said that, they probably would have been lepers for the rest of their lives. But the Bible says, **...as they went, they were cleansed.** They acted on the words of Jesus, as

He was calling things that were not. *As they went*, they were calling things that were not, by their actions.

Every time Jesus told a cripple to take up his bed and walk, He was calling things that were not, as though they were. (John 5:8; Luke 5:24.)

We know a cripple can't walk, and Jesus knew a cripple couldn't walk and carry his bed. *Jesus called them healed when they were bedfast.* The individuals called themselves healed by their actions.

Again in Luke 6:10, Jesus tells a man with a withered hand to stretch forth his hand. A withered hand can't be stretched forth unless it is healed. When the man acted on Jesus' words, he was calling his hand normal. This was God's method and Jesus used it.

Three Methods of Calling Things

There are three main methods of calling things that are not. You can call things that are not *by praying the answer.* You can call things that are not *by confession of the Word of God.*

You can call things that are not *by your actions.*
The lepers and the crippled man were actually
calling things that were not by their actions.

*Speaking the end results is a method of calling
things that are not.* Jesus continually operated
in this principle.

*You must continue to practice this principle if
you are to develop in it.* It takes time, it doesn't
come overnight. You have to discipline yourself
to believe the things that you say will come to
pass. You can't talk all kinds of foolishness day
after day and develop in this principle.

A New Way of Life

Because it is so important for you to begin
now to call things that are not, I have included
this confession to jump-start your faith.

*(Read out loud and declare these truths
with a loud voice.)*

***

Heavenly Father, I covenant with you now
to always give voice to Your Word and never
give voice to the words of the enemy. I declare

52

that I am the redeemed of the Lord and I have been delivered from the powers of darkness. I am redeemed from sickness. I am redeemed from poverty and I am redeemed from spiritual death. Therefore, I forbid sickness or disease to operate in my body for my body is the temple of the Holy Ghost.

***

Body, I am speaking to you! I charge you in the name of the Lord Jesus Christ and by the authority of the Holy Word that you are healed and made whole in Jesus name. Galatians 3:13 is flowing in my bloodstream, transforming my body and causing it to conform to the Word of God.

***

I am far from oppression and fear does not come near me. No weapon that is formed against me will prosper, but whatever I do will prosper! I boldly declare that I will walk in prosperity. I will walk in health, and peace of mind, for Your Word causes me to prevail.[3]

---

[3] Compiled from God's Creative Power® by Charles Capps

For a complete list of CDs, DVDs, and books
by Capps Ministries, write:

Capps Ministries
P.O. Box 10, Broken Arrow, Oklahoma 74013

Toll Free Order Line (24 hours)
1-877-396-9400

E-Books
& MP3's
Available

www.cappsministries.com
Visit us online for:

Radio Broadcasts in Your Area
Concepts of Faith Television Broadcast listings:
Local Stations, **Daystar**, **VICTORY**, & **TCT** Television Network

youtube.com/CappsMinistries
facebook.com/CharlesCappsMinistries

BOOKS BY CHARLES CAPPS
AND ANNETTE CAPPS

Angels

God's Creative Power® for Finances
(Also available in Spanish)

God's Creative Power® - Gift Edition
(Also available in Spanish)

BOOKS BY ANNETTE CAPPS

Quantum Faith®
(Also available in Spanish)

*Reverse The Curse in
Your Body and Emotions*

Removing the Roadblocks to Health and Healing

Overcoming Persecution

BOOKS BY CHARLES CAPPS

Calling Things That Are Not

Triumph Over The Enemy

When Jesus Prays Through You

The Tongue – A Creative Force

Releasing the Ability of God Through Prayer

End Time Events

Authority in Three Worlds

Changing the Seen and Shaping The Unseen

Faith That Will Not Change

Faith and Confession

God's Creative Power® Will Work For You
(Also available in Spanish)

God's Creative Power® For Healing
(Also available in Spanish)

Success Motivation Through the Word

God's Image of You

Seedtime and Harvest
(Also available in Spanish)

The Thermostat of Hope
(Also available in Spanish)

How You Can Avoid Tragedy

Kicking Over Sacred Cows

The Substance of Things

The Light of Life in the Spirit of Man

Faith That Will Work For You

Charles Capps a farmer from England, Arkansas became an internationally known Bible teacher by sharing practical truths from the Word of God. His simplistic, down to earth style of applying spiritual principles to daily  life has appealed to people from every Christian denomination.

The requests for speaking engagements became so great after the printing of *God's Creative Power® Will Work for You©* that he retired from farming and became a full-time Bible teacher. His books are available in multiple languages throughout the world.

Besides publishing 24 books, including best-sellers *The Tongue A Creative Force and God's Creative Power®* series which has sold over 7 million copies, Capps Ministries has a national daily radio broadcast and weekly TV broadcast called "Concepts of Faith".